The Statue of Liberty

by Kevin Blake

Consultant:
Barry Moreno, Historian and Librarian
The Statue of Liberty National Monument and
The Ellis Island National Museum of Immigration

BEARPORT
PUBLISHING

New York, New York

Credits

Cover, © holbox/Shutterstock; 2–3, © Zarnell/Shutterstock; 4, © Granger, NYC; 4TL, © Matt Trommer/Shutterstock; 4BL, © Matt Trommer/Shutterstock; 5, tinyurl.com/gqkkcuh/Public Domain; 6L, Library of Congress; 6R, tinyurl.com/hw8y5zs/Public Domain; 7, © Granger, NYC; 7L, tinyurl.com/hszpllb/Public Domain; 8L, © Loolee/Alamy; 8R, © iStockphoto/SJVictrix; 9T, © Ang Wee Heng John/Dreamstime; 9BL, © Granger, NYC; 9BR, © Joshua Haviv/Shutterstock; 10, NYPL/Public Domain; 11, tinyurl.com/ljtupw6/Public Domain; 12, © North Wind Picture Archives/Alamy; 13L, NYPL/Public Domain; 13R, © North Wind Picture Archives/Alamy; 14L, U.S. National Park Service; 14R, tinyurl.com/jubceh6/Public Domain; 15, © PRISMA ARCHIVO/Alamy; 16T, © Everett Collection Historical/Alamy; 16B, © Hemis/Alamy; 17, Library of Congress; 17R, Library of Congress; 18, © ChameleonsEye/Shutterstock; 19L, Library of Congress; 19R, tinyurl.com/zrrycbd/Public Domain; 20L, The Jefferson R. Burdick Collection, Gift of Jefferson R. Burdick; 20R, © Granger NYC; 21, National Park Service, Statue of Liberty NM; 22, © North Wind Picture Archives/Alamy; 23L, National Park Service, Statue of Liberty NM; 23R, © Everett Historical/Shutterstock; 24, © Everett Historical/Shutterstock; 25, NYPL/Public Domain; 26TL, © Yuri Samsonov/Shutterstock; 26BL, © Etraveler/Dreamstime; 26R, National Park Service, Statue of Liberty NM; 27, © holbox/Shutterstock; 28, © Josef Hanus/Shutterstock; 29, © Josef Hanus/Shutterstock; 31, © Chris Parypa Photography/Shutterstock; 32, © Chris Parypa Photography/Shutterstock.

Publisher: Kenn Goin
Senior Editor: Joyce Tavolacci
Creative Director: Spencer Brinker
Design: The Design Lab
Photo Researcher: Editorial Directions, Inc.

Library of Congress Cataloging-in-Publication Data

Names: Blake, Kevin, 1978– author.
Title: The Statue of Liberty / by Kevin Blake.
Description: New York, New York : Bearport Publishing, 2017. | Series: American places: from vision to reality | Includes bibliographical references and index. | Audience: 7–12._
Identifiers: LCCN 2016012324 (print) | LCCN 2016012840 (ebook) | ISBN 9781944102418 (library binding : alk. paper) | ISBN 9781944997144 (ebook)
Subjects: LCSH: Statue of Liberty (New York, N.Y.)—Juvenile literature. | New York (N.Y.)—Buildings, structures, etc.—Juvenile literature.
Classification: LCC F128.64.L6 B55 2017 (print) | LCC F128.64.L6 (ebook) | DDC 974.7—dc23
LC record available at http://lccn.loc.gov/2016012324

For more information, write to Bearport Publishing Company, Inc., 45 West 21st Street, Suite 3B, New York, New York 10010. Printed in the United States of America.

10 9 8 7 6 5 4 3 2 1

Contents

Liberty's Birthday

On a wet October day in 1886, more than one million people jammed the streets of New York City. They had gathered to cheer on a parade **presided** over by President Grover Cleveland. Throughout the busy city, bands played **patriotic** songs and people eagerly waved American and French flags. Even the rain couldn't stop the excitement.

The parade moving down a street called Broadway in New York City on October 28, 1886

As the parade reached the southern tip of the city, onlookers could see a giant metal object rising out of New York **Harbor**. It stood more than 300 feet (91 m) tall and was topped with a glowing **torch**. A huge French flag covered the upper part of it. Suddenly, the flag was pulled away revealing the Statue of Liberty to the crowd. People wept with joy and shouted in delight. They had never seen anything so beautiful.

Boats filled with people crowded New York Harbor to see the statue.

The statue's official name was *Liberty Enlightening the World*, but most people called it the Statue of Liberty.

Dreaming Big

Where had the majestic statue come from, and who had built it? Edouard de Laboulaye, a French law professor, first dreamt up the idea to build the **monument**. Edouard admired American **democracy** because people were free to choose their leaders. In France, where Edouard lived, the people didn't have a choice. So Edouard had an idea—France should build a huge monument in the United States that celebrated democracy and liberty. Maybe it would inspire the French people to create their own democracy!

Edouard deeply respected President Abraham Lincoln, who fought to end slavery and keep America united and free.

Edouard de Laboulaye

During the Revolutionary War (1775–1783), America fought for independence from Great Britain. France was America's biggest **ally** and helped the Americans win the war.

Edouard told his friend, a young French sculptor named Auguste Bartholdi, about the idea. Auguste agreed to design and build a giant statue. The young sculptor did not realize, however, just how much hard work was to come.

According to one story, Edouard first told Auguste (above) about his idea for a monument at a dinner party.

Auguste Bartholdi in his studio

The Design

Auguste quickly went to work on his design. It wasn't easy, however. How could a statue represent the idea of liberty? After a lot of thought, Auguste decided to model the statue after *Libertas*, the Roman **goddess** of freedom. Like *Libertas*, the new statue would look like a woman and wear a flowing gown called a *stola*.

An ancient Roman coin showing the goddess, *Libertas*

A statue of a Roman goddess wearing a *stola*

Auguste wanted the statue to represent liberty in other ways, too. So he designed a glowing torch—a **symbol** of **enlightenment** and freedom—for the statue to hold. His plan also included broken chains, symbolizing the end of **oppression**, at the statue's feet. In her left hand, Auguste would place a tablet with the date July 4, 1776—America's Independence Day—written on it.

The tablet with the date, July 4, 1776, written in Roman numerals

Some people think Auguste modeled the statue's face after his mother, Charlotte.

Charlotte Bartholdi

Finding the Perfect Spot

After the design was complete, Auguste needed to find a place to put the statue. In 1871, he sailed from France to America to **scout** locations. When his ship entered New York Harbor, Auguste's eyes landed on the perfect spot. It was a small, rocky piece of land near Manhattan called Bedloe's Island. What better place to put Lady Liberty, Auguste thought, than at the gateway to America!

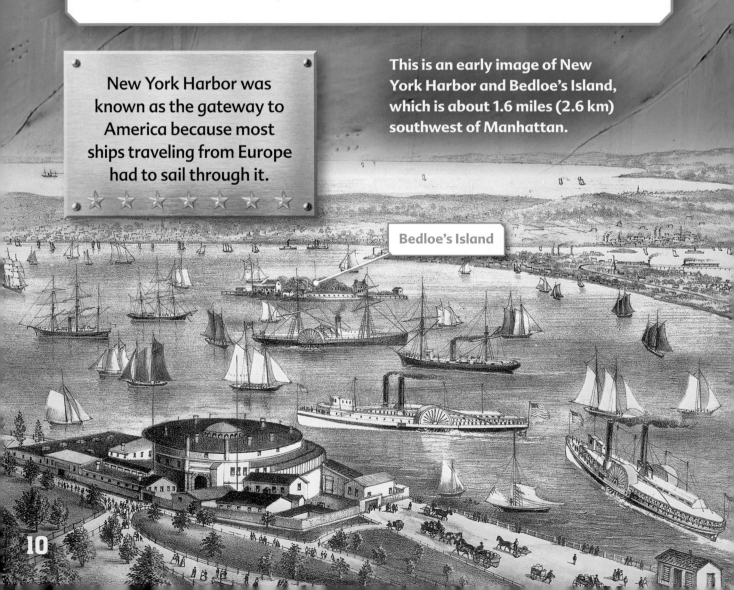

New York Harbor was known as the gateway to America because most ships traveling from Europe had to sail through it.

This is an early image of New York Harbor and Bedloe's Island, which is about 1.6 miles (2.6 km) southwest of Manhattan.

Bedloe's Island

However, Auguste needed money and support from the American people to build the statue and to use Bedloe's Island. So he toured the country and met with Americans to ask for help. Auguste even spoke with President Ulysses S. Grant. The president liked Auguste's idea but wouldn't give him any money or make any promises just yet. Auguste would have to keep working to build support for the huge statue.

Ulysses S. Grant was President of the United States from 1869 to 1877.

The World's Fair

Auguste came up with a brilliant plan to create excitement and raise money for the statue. A huge festival called the U.S. Centennial Exposition, or World's Fair, was being held in Philadelphia in 1876. He knew there wasn't enough time to build the entire statue to display at the fair, but he could construct a small part of it. This would be his chance to show Americans just how amazing the statue would be.

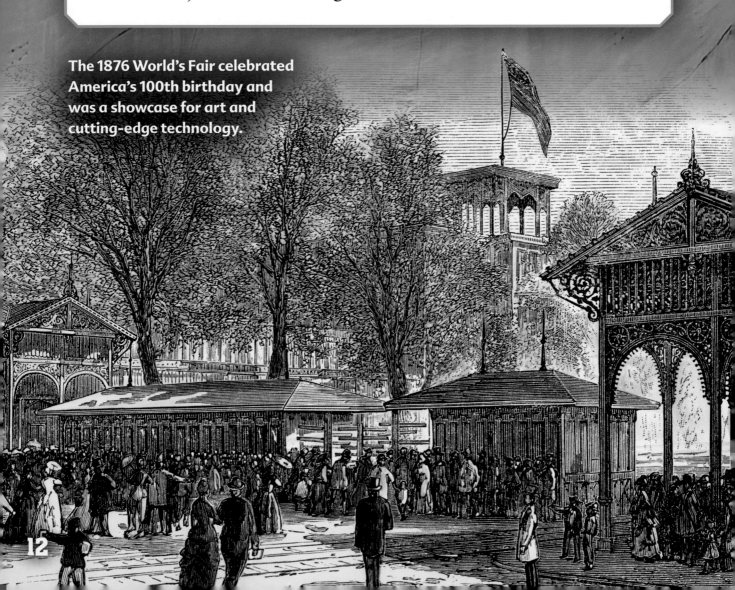

The 1876 World's Fair celebrated America's 100th birthday and was a showcase for art and cutting-edge technology.

For the fair, Auguste decided to make one of the statue's hands and the torch. Back in France, his team of craftsmen built a **plaster** model and covered it with a wood frame. Then they heated sheets of copper—a strong, lightweight metal—until it softened. The workers hammered the soft copper sheets over the wooden frame. As the copper cooled, it hardened. When completed, the hand and torch stood as tall as a three-story building and was big enough to fit a staircase inside!

Workers shape thin sheets of copper using a wooden frame.

In the 1800s, most statues were built out of marble or another kind of stone. Stone, however, would be too heavy and expensive for Auguste's statue.

A drawing of Auguste's hand and torch

13

Building Excitement

The giant copper hand and torch became a main **attraction** at the World's Fair. For fifty cents, visitors climbed the stairs inside the hand to reach the torch. Near the display, Auguste placed a drawing of what the completed statue would look like. Visitors **marveled** at the sight of the beautiful, **colossal** figure.

Auguste's sketch of the completed statue

The finished hand and torch

Roughly 9 million people came to the World's Fair in 1876. At that time, there were only about 50 million people living in the United States!

Soon, excitement for the statue spread throughout America. In 1877, Congress voted to allow Auguste to use Bedloe's Island. In addition, France and the United States agreed to split the cost of building the monument. The French would pay for the statue, while the Americans would cover the cost of constructing a huge **pedestal** for it to stand on. Auguste was thrilled. He could now finish his work.

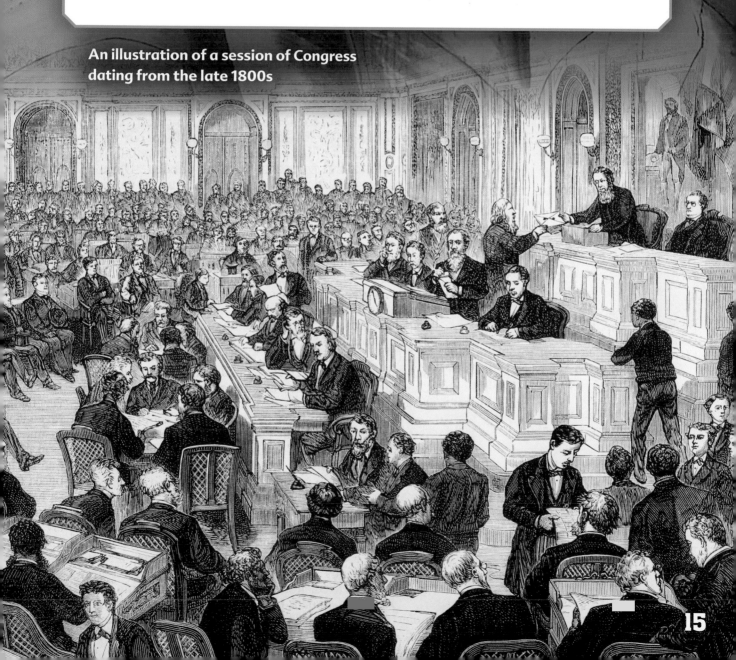

An illustration of a session of Congress dating from the late 1800s

Supporting the Statue

There was still something important that Auguste had yet to figure out. How could he build a giant statue that wouldn't **topple** over? Copper was a great material for the exterior, but it wasn't strong enough to support the enormous figure. Auguste returned to France and asked a young French **engineer** named Gustave Eiffel for help.

Sculptors prepare the wooden frame for the left arm.

This photo shows the same arm after copper has been applied to it.

Gustave suggested putting sturdy iron beams inside the statue. The hard metal would be strong enough to hold up the statue the same way bones hold up a body. Auguste liked the idea. Using 250,000 pounds (113,398 kg) of iron, French workers built the skeleton. The statue was quickly taking shape.

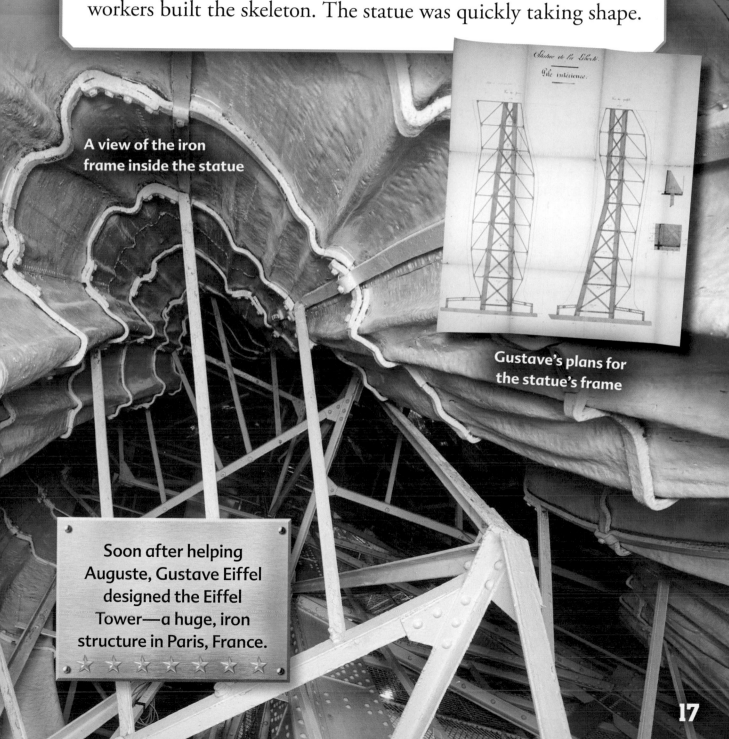

A view of the iron frame inside the statue

Gustave's plans for the statue's frame

Soon after helping Auguste, Gustave Eiffel designed the Eiffel Tower—a huge, iron structure in Paris, France.

A Huge Pedestal

Back in America, work on the statue's pedestal was moving slowly. Richard Morris Hunt, the **architect** chosen to design it, faced some big challenges. For one thing, the pedestal had to be large and strong enough to support the weight of the 450,000-pound (204,117 kg) statue. To solve this problem, Richard designed an 89-foot (27 m) tall **concrete** pedestal with 20-foot (6 m) thick walls covered with a type of stone called granite.

The pedestal had to be big enough to accommodate the statue's huge feet!

To begin building the **foundation** for the pedestal, workers dug a 15-foot (4.6 m) deep hole on Bedloe's Island. Then they pumped it full of concrete. However, the money set aside for the project by the American Committee for the Statue of Liberty soon ran out. The comittee would need another $100,000 to finish the job. They asked Congress for help, but Congress said no. Without a pedestal, there could be no statue.

A sketch of the pedestal

Architect Richard Morris Hunt was famous for designing houses for wealthy people in the 1800s.

Pulitzer to the Rescue

As time passed, it looked as though the pedestal might never get built. That's when a man named Joseph Pulitzer came to the rescue. Joseph was an **immigrant** from Hungary who owned a famous newspaper called *The World*. He loved what the statue stood for and decided to ask the readers of his newspaper for help.

JOSEPH PULITZER
The New York World.

The front page of
The World newspaper

Joseph printed several articles in which he encouraged ordinary people to donate any amount of money they could afford to give. His **persuasive** writing did the trick. More than 125,000 people—including children—gave small donations of as little as one penny. Soon, there was enough money to finish the pedestal!

With the $100,000 raised, workers were able to finish building the pedestal.

Joseph Pulitzer promised that anyone who contributed money for the pedestal would get his or her name printed in his paper—and he carried out his promise!

Putting It All Together

While the Americans worked on the pedestal, Auguste had to figure out a way to transport the finished statue to New York. Because of its size, it couldn't be sent in one piece. Instead, French workers had to **disassemble** the statue into hundreds of smaller pieces. They carefully packed the pieces into crates and then loaded them onto a ship called the *Isere*.

The *Isere*

Auguste's workers packed and loaded 214 crates onto the ship.

The statue was so big that it took seven trains to haul the crates from Auguste's workshop in Paris to the *Isere*.

In 1885, the *Isere* sailed across the Atlantic Ocean to New York. After unpacking the crates, workers **erected** the iron skeleton on top of the pedestal. Then, while swinging on ropes attached to the towering structure, they fastened the copper pieces to the skeleton using thousands of **rivets**. When they were done, the Statue of Liberty was the tallest man-made structure in the United States. "The dream of my life is accomplished!" declared Auguste.

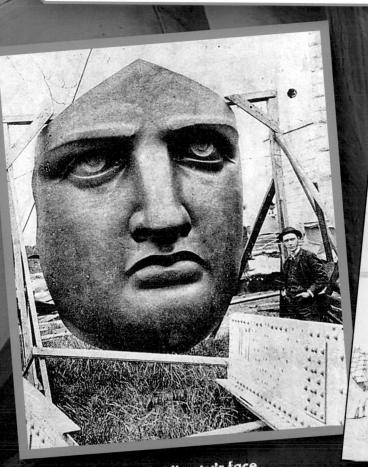

Lady Liberty's face

Brave Statue of Liberty workers swung from ropes hundreds of feet in the air.

The Immigrant's Statue

In October 1886, the Statue of Liberty was **unveiled** to the public during a huge celebration. As Edouard de Laboulaye and Auguste had hoped, the statue was a beautiful symbol of American freedom. It was that very freedom that encouraged millions of immigrants from all over the world to sail to New York City and start a new life in the United States. For many, the Statue of Liberty was the first thing they saw when they arrived in their new home.

Most immigrants came to America to escape poverty and to freely practice their religion.

Emma Lazarus wrote a famous poem about the millions of immigrants who passed by Lady Liberty. The poem was **inscribed** on the statue's pedestal in 1903.

In 1890, the U.S. government built an immigration station on Ellis Island—not far from the statue. Immigrants were required to stop at Ellis Island for questioning and a brief medical examination before they were allowed to enter the country. In the early 1900s, more than 5,000 immigrants passed by the Statue of Liberty on their way to Ellis Island each day!

More than 12 million immigrants entered the United Stated through Ellis Island between 1892 and 1954.

Lady Liberty Today

Over time, water has changed the Statue of Liberty's color from the reddish brown of a copper penny to a bluish green. In 1984, two years before the statue's 100th birthday, Lady Liberty underwent a major **restoration**. Workers repaired holes in her copper skin and replaced the rusting iron framework. The torch, which had been badly damaged by seawater, was replaced with a **replica**.

Images of the Statue of Liberty can be found on coins, stamps, license plates, and even in movies!

Scaffolding used during the 1984 restoration

Today, nearly four million people from around the world visit the statue each year. Some even climb up the 354 steps to the statue's crown. When they reach the top, visitors can peer through tiny windows. There, they are rewarded with an amazing view that goes on for miles and miles.

The Statue of Liberty

BY THE NUMBERS

Distance Between Eyes: 2 feet 6 inches (0.8 m)

Length of Nose: 4 feet 6 inches (1.4 m)

Width of Mouth: 3 feet (0.9 m)

Height of Face: 8 feet (2.4 m)

Total Height: 305 feet 6 inches (93 m) from the base of the foundation to the tip of the torch

Each year, hundreds of bolts of lightning strike the statue.

There are 25 windows in the crown.

Length of Index Finger: 8 feet (2.4 m)

Weight: 450,000 pounds (204,117 kg)

Thickness of Copper Covering: 3/32 of an inch (2.4 mm) —or less than the thickness of two pennies!

Waist: 35 feet (10.7 m)

If the Statue of Liberty wore shoes, her shoe size would be 879!

Glossary

ally (AL-eye) a country that gives support to another country

architect (AR-kih-tekt) a person who designs buildings

attraction (uh-TRAK-shuhn) something that draws people's interest

colossal (kuh-LOSS-uhl) very large

concrete (kon-KREET) a mixture of sand, water, cement, and gravel

democracy (dih-MOK-ruh-see) a form of government in which people choose their leaders

disassemble (dis-uh-SEM-buhl) to take apart or break into pieces

engineer (en-juh-NIHR) a person who designs and constructs buildings, machines, roads, and bridges

enlightenment (en-LITE-uhn-muhnt) the state of having knowledge or understanding

erected (ih-REKT-id) built something

foundation (foun-DAY-shuhn) a solid structure on which something sits

goddess (GOD-iss) a female god

harbor (HAR-bur) a protected body of water where ships can unload goods

immigrant (IM-uh-gruhnt) a person who comes from one country to live permanently in a new one

inscribed (in-SKRIBED) carved a written message into something

marveled (MAHR-vuhld) viewed with amazement

monument (MAHN-yuh-muhnt) a statue or structure built to remember something

oppression (uh-PRESH-uhn) the use of authority or power in a cruel or unfair way

patriotic (pay-tree-AH-tik) loving one's country

pedestal (PED-*uh*-stuhl) a support for a statue or column

persuasive (per-SWAY-siv) something that convinces people to change their minds

plaster (PLAS-tur) a mixture of water and tiny bits of rock

presided (pri-ZIDE-uhd) to be in charge of something

replica (REP-li-kuh) an exact copy

restoration (RESS-tuh-ray-shuhn) the act of bringing something back to its original condition

rivets (RIV-its) metal pins used to hold metal pieces together

scout (SKOWT) to search for something

symbol (SIM-buhl) something that stands for something else

topple (TOP-uhl) to fall over

torch (TORCH) a flaming light

unveiled (uhn-VAYLD) uncovered

Bibliography

Khan, Yasmin Sabina. *Enlightening the World: The Creation of the Statue of Liberty.* Ithaca, NY: Cornell University Press (2010).

Mitchell, Elizabeth. *Liberty's Torch: The Great Adventure to Build the Statue of Liberty.* New York: Atlantic Monthly Press (2014).

The National Park Service: www.nps.gov/stli/index.htm

Read More

Demuth, Patricia Brennen. *What Was Ellis Island?* New York: Grosset & Dunlap (2014).

Holub, Joan. *What Is the Statue of Liberty?* New York: Grosset & Dunlap (2014).

Landau, Elaine. *The Statue of Liberty (True Books).* New York: Children's Press (2008).

Learn More Online

To learn more about the Statue of Liberty, visit:
www.bearportpublishing.com/AmericanPlaces

Index

About the Author

Kevin Blake lives in Providence, Rhode Island, with his wife, Melissa, and son, Sam. When he was little, his great-grandmother told him about how she sailed past the Statue of Liberty on her way to her new home in America.